TODAY'S DEACON

TODAY'S DEACON
Contemporary Issues and Cross-Currents

The National Association of Diaconate Directors
Keynote Addresses, 2005

By
Alfred C. Hughes,
Frederick F. Campbell,
and William T. Ditewig

With responses by
Michael Kennedy, Owen F. Cummings,
and Marti R. Jewell

Paulist Press
New York/Mahwah, N.J.

Cover design by Cynthia Dunne
Book design by Lynn Else

Library of Congress Cataloging-in-Publication Data

National Association of Diaconate Directors. Convention (2005 : New Orleans, La.)
    Today's deacon : contemporary issues and cross-currents : the National Association of Diaconate Directors keynote addresses, 2005 / by Alfred C. Hughes, Frederick F. Campbell, and William T. Ditewig ; with responses by Michael Kennedy, Owen F. Cummings, and Marti R. Jewell.
        p.   cm.
    Includes bibliographical references.
    ISBN 0-8091-4399-2 (alk. paper)
    1. Deacons—Catholic Church—Congresses. I. Hughes, Alfred Clifton, 1932-   II. Campbell, Frederick F. III. Ditewig, William T. IV. Kennedy, Michael. V. Cummings, Owen F. VI. Jewell, Marti R. VII. Title.
BX1912.N27 2005
262′.142—dc22

                                                              2006011941

BX 1912
.N27
2005

Published by Paulist Press
997 Macarthur Boulevard
Mahwah, New Jersey 07430

www.paulistpress.com

Printed and bound in the
United States of America

0672402225

Contents

Contents

A Note of Introduction

Deacon Daniel L. Peterson
President
National Association of Diaconate Directors

God blessed us with a great convention in April 2005, and the hospitality of the New Orleans deacons was unsurpassable. Unfortunately, as I write this, the people of this great city and other coastal areas of Louisiana, Alabama, and Mississippi are contemplating recovery from the tragic destruction and flooding of Hurricane Katrina. It may be years before life returns to normal in those ravaged areas. Our thoughts and prayers go out to those affected by this storm and its aftermath.

This publication contains the keynotes of the National Association of Diaconate Directors (NADD) Convention 2005 held at the Omni Royal Orleans Hotel in New Orleans. These works cover two distinct topics: Restorative Justice and the new publication *National Directory for the Formation, Ministry and Life of Permanent Deacons in the United States* (a.k.a. the *National Directory*).

A Note of Introduction

The keynote on Restorative Justice was presented by the Most Reverend Alfred C. Hughes, Archbishop of New Orleans. The bishops of Louisiana have embraced Restorative Justice as the best means of permanent rehabilitation of those who have been incarcerated, to return them to be productive members of society. Archbishop Hughes discusses his observations on the impact to society of the imprisoned and how Restorative Justice can not only be a useful method of rehabilitation, but one that reflects our Catholic values as well.

The two other keynotes presented in this publication deal with the *National Directory*. Promulgated on December 26, 2004, notably the Feast of Deacon St. Stephen the protomartyr, this document contains the new norms for the lifelong formation of permanent deacons in the United States. As diaconate offices across the country struggle with the details of implementation of this normative document, those "in the know" help us by sharing their insights as to the purpose of the document and *how* deacon directors—those who supervise the formation of deacons—might use this document to redevelop or redefine programs to comply with the new norms.

Most Reverend Frederick F. Campbell, Bishop of Columbus and Chair of the Bishops Committee on the Diaconate (BCD) of the United States Conference of Catholic Bishops (USCCB), shares his thoughts on the impact of the *Directory* and how this new document will affect deacons for years to come.

Daniel L. Peterson

Deacon William T. Ditewig, Executive Director for the Secretariat for the Permanent Diaconate of the BCD, shares his insights in a concise way—with great common sense and good humor—describing suggested methods for implementation of this landmark document.

I trust you will find the following pages enlightening.

Keynote Addresses

Restorative Justice

Most Rev. Alfred C. Hughes, STD
Archbishop of New Orleans

So he told them this parable: "Which one of you, having a hundred sheep and losing one of them, does not leave the ninety-nine in the wilderness and go after the one that is lost until he finds it? When he has found it, he lays it on his shoulders and rejoices. And when he comes home, he calls together his friends and neighbors, saying to them, 'Rejoice with me, for I have found my sheep that was lost.' Just so, I tell you, there will be more joy in heaven over one sinner who repents than over ninety-nine righteous persons who need no repentance." (Luke 15:3–7)

Introduction

Let me begin with a true story. James Townsend was born in Bristol, Pennsylvania, in 1927. His mother was an invalid and was completely bedridden. His father was an alcoholic coal miner who used to beat him up in an effort to toughen him up. Young Jim Townsend began to associate very early in life with tough kids his age or older on the streets. He was first placed in a juvenile prison at eight years of age. By the time he was eighteen years of age, he had spent a total of seven years in prison.

After Jim Townsend emerged from prison for juvenile offenders at eighteen, he married his pregnant girlfriend, Alice Moss. One night, after drinking heavily and getting beaten up over a card game, he went home for a shotgun to "finish off" the men who beat him. His wife, recognizing the implications of what he was proposing to do, scuffled with him, and accidentally the gun went off and killed both Jim's wife and the child in her womb.

Jim Townsend was tried, convicted, and sentenced to prison. While in prison he was plagued with a recurring nightmare. He would see his wife holding their baby. The wife merely stared at him. The baby looked quizzically at him and said, "Why, Daddy?"

Jim Townsend is not sure to this day what started him reading the Bible. At the time, it seemed like the only thing he could do to counteract the boredom he experienced. Then he started to attend church services. He thought it would look good on his record. Gradually he began to sense God knocking on the door of his heart. He finally got up the courage to approach the priest chaplain for the sacrament of penance and reconciliation. Restored now to the Eucharist, Jim Townsend became a changed man in prison. He began to help other prisoners open up and then encouraged them to go to the priest chaplain for confession, as well. A new dream replaced the old nightmare. Now his wife would appear to him smiling, and the baby also smiled and said, "I love you, Daddy."

Before his conversion in prison, Jim Townsend had resented the regular walk of the guard down the cell block to check on each prisoner. As he would pass by, Jim would sometimes plot how he might kill him. Only afterward did he discover that that same guard had a practice of offering a Hail Mary for each prisoner that he walked past. Jim now wonders if that repeated Hail Mary won the grace of his conversion.

Jim's sentence was ultimately reduced for good behavior, and he was released from prison. After a few years he presented himself to the Capuchin Friars and became a religious brother. The last I heard of him he was still serving as a chaplain in a prison in Pennsylvania.

The Present Predicament in Our Prison System

It is difficult to find anyone who is happy with our prison system today. Not too long ago the political rallying cry to express toughness on crime was, "Lock them up and throw away the key." A recent syndicated column by Cokie and Steve Roberts was entitled, "Lock Them Up and Throw Away Your Money," referring to the high cost of imprisonment. What we really want to make sure is that we do not just "Lock them up and throw away our Christian principles."

I do not have the very latest statistics. However, these date back only a few years. At that time Louisiana had the highest number of incarcerated per capita of all states in our country. The adult prison population was approaching 36,000. Of these, 3,400 were serving life sentences; 82 were on death row. (Nearly one-tenth are either to be executed or spend their whole lives in prison.)

In addition, there is a significant adult population on probation, another 36,000, and 22,000 on parole. If we were to total these three figures, there are some 93,000 people under the supervision of our Louisiana correction system. This does not include the almost 3,000 *federal* prison inmates in Louisiana.

Unfortunately, the prison population is not restricted to adults. The juvenile population totals more than 8,000.

In Louisiana alone, the 2001–02 budget for the Department of Corrections was $583 million.

In a recent syndicated column, William Raspberry reports statistics from the Bureau of Justice that within the past year there has been an increase in our prison and jail population of 3.7 percent in the United States. There is also a reported decrease in the amount of crime. Some would suggest that the increase in imprisonment has brought about a diminishment in crime. But the Washington-based Justice Policy Institute has done an analysis of the patterns in different parts of the country. Paradoxically, in those sections of the country where there has been a decline in prison population, there has also been a decline in homicides. In those parts of the country, especially the South and the West, where there has been an increase in prison population, there has also been an increase in homicides. The question then is legitimately raised: Is our present approach to the punishment of crime what God wants us to do?

Restorative Justice

The Bishops of the United States are urging us to explore together whether God is asking us to adopt a new way of thinking and acting. Drawing on our scriptural, theological, and sacramental heritage, we have issued a pastoral statement entitled *Responsibility, Rehabilitation and Restoration* to outline an approach to crime and punishment. Interestingly, this approach is not unlike the moral vision of the human person in society that originally inspired the prison system in the United States. This vision was and is called *Restorative Justice*. Restorative justice is not retributive justice; nor is it penal justice. Restorative justice seeks to repair the violated social order by leading the offenders to repentance, reparation, and penance and the victim to healing and the freedom to forgive. Restorative justice recognizes that there is a right order in our society that promotes the common good. When that right order is violated, redress should be available to those who are victims and restitution is incumbent upon those responsible. Let us look first at the role of the offender, then that of the victim, and finally that of society as a whole.

The offender is the one who is responsible for the violation of the right order. The most important task for the offender is to recognize his fault, to repent of his wrong doing, to accept punishment, and to engage in whatever restitution may be realistically possible. Please note how closely this follows the church's teaching with regard to sin, repentance, confession, acceptance of penance, and restitution. We call this *responsibility*.

Victims are an integral part of the experience of crime. When the criminal system marginalizes the role of victims, their hurt can often turn to anger and the desire for revenge. The violation that victims have experienced calls for justice. This is the intended purpose of our justice system, providing for objective trials, including a trial by jury if so chosen. But just punishment alone will not bring healing to the victim.

As the pastoral statement of the Louisiana Catholic Bishops states in its very title, *Let Justice and Mercy Meet,* victims will not be healed until they are helped to move toward forgiveness. There is a great deal of confusion about the gospel call to forgiveness. Many victims feel that forgiveness is only reasonable if repentance on the part of the offender has already taken place. How can we forgive someone who is unwilling to be forgiven? Christ's example on the cross is our model. He has offered to us the grace of forgiveness. That forgiveness, however, does not effect our salvation unless we accept his offer and respond appropriately. So it is in our dealings with one another. The offer of forgiveness frees the aggrieved party—an example is Pope John

Paul II with his would-be assassin Mehmet Ali Acqa in December 1983. Let us be clear that the person who has offended receives forgiveness only if repentance takes place. Although it may not be possible for this to happen frequently, it can be a great grace when victim and offender are brought together so that forgiveness can be offered and repentance expressed. There is nothing more healing than this. It is what we call *reconciliation*. Please note that this is what the sacrament of penance and reconciliation makes possible for us in our relationship to God.

In addition to addressing the role of offenders and victims, the Catholic tradition has always recognized the importance of the social order violated by crime. The right order has been violated. Right order must be redressed by appropriate punishment. Again, some are confused that forgiveness suggests that there is now no need for punishment. Let us again remember our Catholic teaching. In the sacrament of penance, God forgives us, but our acceptance of a penance is our recognition of the need for temporal punishment for our sins. The guilt is removed. The need to do satisfaction for our sin is not. This is the role of punishment in society. Obviously, the selection of the punishment should be proportionate to the crime that has been committed. The Christian view of punishment is not so much *punitive* as it is *rehabilitative*. If the punishment is geared to help a person move beyond criminal behavior, to adapt a new way of life, then both restoration to the community becomes more possible and the risk of recidivist behavior diminished. The ultimate hope of responsibly chosen punishment is restoration to society with a significantly reduced risk of danger to those who may be further potential victims.

This vision of restorative justice focuses on the responsibility that must be assumed by the offender, justice and reconciliation for the victim, and rehabilitation and restoration for the righting of the social order. Hence, the title for the United States Bishops' pastoral statement: *Responsibility, Rehabilitation and Restoration.*

Is *restorative justice* possible? Is it too idealistic? We need to acknowledge that in this life there is never going to be *full* justice. We will have to wait for full justice in the life to come. But, the issue is, What is the controlling paradigm for our attempts at approximating full justice in this world? What is the goal against which we can measure our efforts? Is that goal retributive justice (an eye for an eye) or penal justice (focus on punishment without concern for rehabilitation) or *restorative justice*?

The Church's Recent Experience with Scandal

No one of us gathered here will deny that the last three years have been extremely difficult for our church. In addressing sin and crime and the appropriate response to it, there is no question but that serious sin and criminal behavior have taken place. What is not fully realized is the extent to which the church has been engaged in her own attempt to model restorative justice. I hope this will be publicly reported one day. We have examined our conscience. We have made a public report confessing the unconscionable activity. We have cooperated with civil authorities in addressing any criminal dimensions. We have attempted to move into restitution for those harmed.

It has not always been easy for victims to experience that justice has been accomplished, especially in cases that date back so far and have had a lingering deleterious effect in their lives. These cases are subject to the statute of limitations and do not allow for judicial proceedings. The establishment, however, of a victims assistance program and the offer of the bishop to meet with victims to assist in healing are initiatives intended to assist in the process of reconciliation. Hopefully, they will also make forgiveness possible. Ultimately, healing will be realized only to the extent that forgiveness becomes a reality.

In an attempt to right the wronged social order, the development of policies for the right handling of these cases, the procedures for education and formation of safe environment programs, and the commitment to complete cooperation with civil authorities have been significant developments. How has this experiment in restorative justice worked? The effectiveness of these efforts will be best assessed in the future, but at the present time I can testify in the case of at least the Archdiocese of New Orleans that we know of no case dating any later than 1992. It is my genuine hope that this positive experience in restorative justice will one day be told and its implications drawn out for a wider society.

As I conclude, may I draw your attention to page 4 of the Louisiana Catholic Bishops' statement, *Let Justice and Mercy Meet*. Here you will find a series of proposals that the bishops are making. These proposals are concrete suggestions for discussion of ways that we in the church in Louisiana and in the wider community might take steps that help us to realize together how best to address crime, punishment, and the common good in light of sacred scripture and Catholic teaching. They have been made only after considerable consultation with significant persons touched by our criminal system. God grant that we can, through education, persuasion, and policy initiatives begin to take some steps together to realize even in this life a fuller measure of God's justice and mercy.

The Impact of the *New National Directory for the Formation, Ministry and Life of Permanent Deacons in the United States*

Most Rev. Frederick F. Campbell
Bishop of Columbus

It is very exciting for me to be here today with you. I am sorry that I cannot be with you over a longer period. My becoming chair of the Bishop's Committee for the Permanent Diaconate coincided with Rome's decision to transfer me to the Diocese of Columbus. And I realized that when I got to Columbus that I was actually working with two different calendars, one that they gave me the day after my installation, and the one that I brought with me that included many of the dates involving the national conference. So I do apologize for the fact that I cannot be with you any longer, although I do find it mildly ironic that I come to New

Orleans for the first time in my life and I meet so many people I know. This is wonderful.

I should like, in the time that I have with you, to talk a little about the *National Directory,* not to go though it line by line, chapter by chapter, or even to talk about it as an instrument for formation and as a diaconate formation program; but rather to talk about some of the larger issues that are raised throughout the *Directory* that I think we should keep in the back of our minds as we prepare to implement it in the dioceses of the United States.

I have worked with the permanent diaconate program since 1978. I was asked by the archbishop while I was still a seminarian to become part of the faculty in the first diaconate program in the Archdiocese of St. Paul and Minneapolis. There were a lot of fresh faces as I look back now. I suspect we did not know what we were doing because there had not been an extraordinary amount of time, work, and experience since that modest paragraph 29 in *Lumen gentium* in which the Council fathers suggested that we might consider reestablishing the diaconate as a permanent order. As we began work with the diaconal program at that point, there was an ongoing attempt to figure out exactly how a permanent deacon fits into the life of the church. How that was to be shaped. How that was to be explained. I think some people at first thought, "Boy, this is a neat idea." And then only later thought, "Well, what do they *do* once they are ordained?"

A little later I worked with another program in the Diocese of Duluth. I got involved with the Diaconate Program of the Diocese of Duluth some fifteen years ago now. That was kind of my intermediate period when the program became a little more carefully shaped. It was maybe four years ago that I was talking with Archbishop Flynn at a table with Bishop Shnurr, and Bishop Shnurr mentioned to me, "Well, you'll be up this weekend for the Diaconate Program." And Archbishop Flynn said, "Do you work in *their* Diaconate Program?" I said, "I have for years, Archbishop." And he said, "Not in ours?" I said, "Well, not yet."

We are at a point where I think there is a fairly clear idea about how a deacon is to be formed, what the requirements of the program are, and how the deacon fits into the church. I think, however, there is still a little confusion about the role of the deacon. I want to say a little more about that later.

I look at the *National Directory* and I notice that the title of my talk was to be "The Impact of the *New Directory* in the United States in the Catholic Church." I understand that there are various overall impacts that are going to emerge from this. We have to realize that the *National Directory* is intended for bishops and for directors of diaconal programs. This was *not* put together and published as a kind of general document or theology of the diaconate. Its immediate impact, I think, is going to be on those bishops who have an instrument by which to reevaluate a program that may already be in place or for those bishops who do not have a program in place and who want to know where to begin. Immediately I think that is one of the greatest impacts that is going to be made.

Second, I think that this *Directory* represents a kind of distillation of the wisdom that has been gained from the past experience, from some things that worked, and some things that did not. There is a clear understanding now of just what the deacon is called to do—at least an understanding on the part of the hierarchy. And, I hope, on the part of the members of the diaconate program. This *Directory* is going to become a blueprint, not only for the formation of permanent deacons, but also a blueprint for their life in ministry. I think it will be a document that will be more and more referred to. There is a greater and stronger specific intention in this document. As you read it, you may notice that instead of saying that deacons should be educated in scripture, doctrine, and so forth, there is quite a long list of what a deacon should do, especially if the deacon has been given faculties to preach.

Way back in the late 1970s, when the program was beginning, I expressed some hesitation about recommending some of the diaconal candidates for faculties to preach because there was a kind of weakness in the early program regarding the study of scripture. I was told, "Don't worry about that. They are going to preach from their experience." Then I hoped we would have a program that would examine their experience! I think there is a clearer understanding now of what preparation has to come about, what the requirements for preaching are. I use that just as an example.

Most Rev. Frederick F. Campbell

The last general impact I think that you are going to have with this *Directory* is on the criteria for admission to a process, on the matter of discernment, and the quality of formation. I think that for a while we were thrashing about asking ourselves, *What are we looking for? What does the church need and require? What are the various human and psychological aspects of a person's personality that are necessary as a foundation for the diaconal process?*

Those, I think, are the sum of the characteristics of the *Directory* that will have a fairly large impact—if used. Now this *Directory* is for individual bishops. Individual bishops have the responsibility for implementing it. I noticed in a paragraph—and I think, Bill [William T. Ditewig], you mentioned it first to me—that if there is a new program developed in the diocese, the bishop is strongly encouraged to submit it for examination at the National Conference. They cannot be required to do so, although the *Directory* is specific to the United States and its norms are to be accepted by all dioceses that are preparing such programs.

Having said that, I want to concentrate on three aspects of the *Directory* that I think are very important, both as specific tasks to which we are called, and also as a general background in which other decisions are going to be made. I will list them very briefly.

The Impact of the New National Directory

1. *The question of what a deacon is.*

I think we, here, who are in the "business" have a general idea of how to answer that. I do not believe it has been really fully expressed within the life of the church.

2. *What is the* diakonia *to which a deacon is called?*

What is that service? What does it look like? How does it shape the life of a deacon? Do we understand that *diakonia* clearly enough?

3. *What is the relationship of the diaconate as a permanent order to the activation of the role of the laity within the church?*

What is that relationship? I think that has to be clarified, although the *Directory* offers a series of hints on how that might be accomplished.

So let me go back to the first question, *What is a deacon?*

Whenever I celebrate the sacrament of confirmation, I threaten to ask the candidate questions. I put it in the form of restoring a tradition that was imposed on me. One of the questions I always pose to them is, "Can you tell me the ranks of the sacrament of Orders?" It was just the other night I said to a young man, "They are standing here before you." And he said, "Oh, there are two. There's a bishop and a priest." I said, "No, there are three." And he said, "No, there's only one priest here." I pointed to the deacon and he said, "Oh, he's a deacon." Now that is emblematic of a difficulty that I think we have within the life of the church. A difficulty understanding what it is that a deacon "is." Not what they "do." But what *is* he? Many people believe that deacons are being ordained because there is a priest shortage. I ask them, "Is that what the church intends: that when we no longer have a priest shortage we stop ordaining deacons, that this is just a stopgap?" There is a strong sense that this is why the church decided to do this. Then I've often asked, "What does a deacon do?" And of course whenever we have a diaconal ordination there is always a list that appears in the local Catholic newspaper that describes what a deacon does. But have you noticed how little is said about what a deacon *is*?

Now when I read over the *Directory,* and I have to say that I am coming in at the tail end of all this work (I'm holding this book in hand and I've had almost nothing to do with putting it together except for reading it over at the conferences, voting "Aye," and waiting patiently for the *recognitio* from Rome), you read through it and you notice that especially in the early chapters, which are not the majority of the *Directory*—though I think they are the most important part of it—there is a increasing stress on the sacramental reality of the deacon. I have had to convince even some deacons that they share in the sacramental reality. I think one of the ongoing challenges of using this directory is to ask ourselves what it means to share in the sacrament of Orders. This means that we first have to ask about the *being* of a deacon before we ask what a deacon *does*.

A deacon, first of all, is not a functionary. They are not being ordained simply to fill gaps in an ecclesiastical bureaucracy. There is a being to the deacon that has to be expressed.

I think most Catholics have almost an intuitive sense of the being of the priest. To a less extent they may have an intuitive sense of the being of the bishop. They are trying to grasp the reality of the deacon. In the *Directory* there are certain emphasis that I think have to be made clear.

First of all, a deacon is ordained and a member of the hierarchy. A deacon is part of the constitution of the church instituted by the will of Christ. The fullness of the church includes the deacon, and the deacon is a part of that fullness of the realization of the church by divine institution. Therefore, a church without the diaconate is a church that is incompletely manifested to the people.

Second, the *Directory* clearly points out that a deacon is conformed to Jesus Christ in a sacramental way. And as conformed to Christ he is an icon of his service. The use of that term *icon* is important. An icon is a representation that actually participates in the reality that it represents. The deacon is an icon of the *diakonia,* the service of Christ. We have to ask ourselves, *What is that service and how does it emerge from sacred scripture and the tradition of the church?*

Third, the diaconate is an order into which men are ordained. They are not ordained deacons as lone rangers. The diaconate is an *order,* and notice that the *Directory* asks bishops to form those structures and to create those opportunities for the diaconate to see itself as an order, a community *directly* under the bishop. I think one of the difficulties early on in many of the diaconal appointments was that these diaconal appointments were almost always made to a *parish*, usually the parish from which they came, and they came to be seen as "junior varsity associates." It is important to reclaim the idea that the deacon is ordained to the diaconate order precisely for service *directly* to the bishop. In the *Directory,* it very clearly says that the diaconate is not an abridged or substitute form of the priesthood. *It is a full order in its own right.* If this is true—and it is—we have to ask ourselves whether we are doing things that obfuscate this reality. Are we assigning deacons or preparing them in a way that *does* make them look like substitute forms of the priesthood, or what the *Directory* calls an abridged priesthood. Regrettably, I think some people see the diaconate as a consolation prize for not being able to be a priest. The *Directory* is very clear in that it also says that in order to establish the distinctiveness of the diaconate order we have to stress the part of that title that sometimes we find merely descriptive of, rather than important for, the order; namely the word *permanent.* The *Directory* says that a deacon ordained to the permanent diaconate should *not* be ordained to the priesthood if widowed. This is a true and permanent order, *not* a transition, no matter how long, to the priesthood. In order to stress the *order* of the diaconate it is going to take some specific work—first of all on the part of the bishop.

Some specific things that a bishop who wishes to implement the *Directory* is going to have to do are to institute a catechesis on the diaconate, even and especially for his own deacons. It is part of the bishop's responsibility to create that catechesis. I think it is also important to learn a little about the history of the diaconate. *How* did the diaconate actually function in the early church? *Why* was it suppressed as the permanent order? There was at one point in the church's history a major confrontation between the presbyterate and the diaconate. Why did this happen? I encourage you to read the letters of the bishop, St. Ignatius of Antioch [died ca. 107]. He has some wonderful things to say about his deacons. He says at one point that you are to receive my deacon as you would receive Jesus Christ himself. At first that may swell us with pride, but then we come to realize what an enormous challenge it is. What did the deacons actually do? How did they live in the community?

My first point is that we have to be clear about what a deacon *is* before we start talking about what a deacon *does*. If we get the order changed around, we are going to be spending some time uselessly arguing over who does what. I think that is very unfortunate.

The second issue then is, *What precisely* is *the service of* diakonia? I noticed that the thrust of the *Directory* was toward the understanding of *diakonia* and service especially to those in need. A first emphasis may be on the poor, but it is also on those in spiritual or psychological need. I go back to sacred scripture and I ask myself, *If the deacon is to perform the* diakonia *of Christ, what was that* diakonia *for Christ?* The first thing I come up with is not the washing of the feet, but rather the complete devotion to the Word of his Heavenly Father in the fulfillment of his wisdom. That is a light that is given over entirely to the revelation of who God is in this world and to following his Word in following his will. This was an obedience even unto death—death on a cross. I think in sacred scripture we can safely say that the greatest act of *diakonia* of Jesus Christ was the cross. It is there that we have to begin in defining what is the "service" that we offer as a deacon. I include myself in this because you may know that whenever a bishop ordains deacons he is encouraged to wear a dalmatic under the chasuble, realizing that it represents the fullness of orders, but also remembering that he is called to live the reality to which he has called these men he is ordaining. But it starts at the cross. It starts at the realization that one life is given over entirety to the manifestation of the love and mercy of God our Heavenly Father. From that sense of manifestation other things follow, such as the service one offers to a friend. You notice that in the description of the washing of the feet at the Last Supper, Jesus immediately follows his explanation of the washing of the feet by saying, "I no longer call you slaves....I have called you friends" (John 15:15 NAB). This is an act not only of *service*. It is an act of *communion*. It is an act of establishing the strongest bonds of friendship. But there is a curiosity to the way that some of the deacons are described in the New Testament. Take, for example, St. Stephen and St. Philip, two of the seven that were ordained. In the Acts of the Apostles, we are told that they were ordained to the service of the table. Now many people think that that is the basis of the *diakonia*, of serving other, of serving a table, helping with whatnot and expanding it to a larger sense. But if you read further in the Acts of the Apostles, do you ever find

Stephen and Philip serving at tables? It's curious that when they are actually acting out of their diaconate they are not serving in the way that we have maybe naively thought. The service of St. Stephen is to conform himself completely to the person of Christ, even to dying as Christ did. I think that's why the description of his martyrdom in the Acts of the Apostles (8:60) is described with the very words that Jesus himself spoke. The whole of Stephen's diaconate seemed to be taken up with his martyrdom—that is his confession—his profession of his faith, and his desire to be conformed completely to Christ.

I find it wonderful that the church has always celebrated the feast of St. Stephen the day after Christmas. As if to say, "Do you understand what it means for Christ to take on our flesh? And the responsibility all flesh now bears to God?" Remember that old Christmas carol, "And Christ was born for this. And Christ was born for this."

Take the indication we have in the work of St. Philip, who converted the Ethiopian eunuch (Acts 8:26–40). It was Philip as an educator. It is significant that from the beginning there seems to have been a sense of diaconal service as education, a call to conversion, and a complete identification of oneself with Christ.

It is from that initial service, then, that I think other things that the deacon does must come. Unless a deacon is in himself a manifestation of the *diakonia* of Christ, no matter what he does or how busy he becomes, he will not be an effective member of the order. In the *Directory* this is very clearly stressed when it says that one of the priorities of a formational process is human and spiritual conversion and formation. As I used to tell the seminarians when they would ask, "What do you look for?" I would say that one of the first things that I look for is, "Is this person serious about the pursuit of holiness and can this person call others to the pursuit of holiness?"

So, in this service from which the other things flow, once we have established this we can honestly ask, "What is the deacon to do?" How does the deacon manifest himself in the church? I think there are many ways in which this *diakonia* of Christ can be established. I had a deacon in one of my parishes—in fact I have always worked with a deacon since I was ordained a priest twenty-five years ago—who was, I think, the quintessence of a diaconal commitment to service. He never wanted to do anything really public. He asked me never to ask him to preach. He said, "I just don't like that. I've done it enough to my kids." But he had an incredible sense of the needs of others. He could go through the parish, or the neighborhood, and he'd pick up the signals. And he'd come to me and he'd say, "Father, I think we need this." Or, "We need that." It got to a point where I never questioned it. He would ask for some money and we always managed to get it. He had an innate nose for need. It was just wonderful—but yet it was so unassuming. Added to this was a wonderful quality of getting others to collaborate, I think by giving them the impression that it was their idea. He was known to be a man of deep prayer. He had a virtue that we do not talk about very much, a virtue that is so important to the diaconate, and that is the virtue of *vigilance,* watchfulness. Now many people assume that vigilance is a negative virtue, that it is a virtue by which we avoid sin. That is certainly a part of it. But the virtue of vigilance is also a looking out, a keen sense of sight or hearing. There is a wonderful picture that is now in one of the Vatican museums that I first saw in Chicago of Mary, Joseph, and the Child Jesus resting on their flight to Egypt. For a painting that was over four hundred years old, it had a powerful realism to it. There is Mary lightly holding the Child with her back up against a tree in utter exhaustion. The picture is of Joseph with one arm around Mary with the other holding up the Christ Child in Mary's weakening arms. What is so remarkable about this picture are Joseph's *eyes*. He is as tired as his spouse, but the eyes are darting here and there, always looking, always reaching out. What a wonderful model, I think, for the *diakonia* of a permanent deacon, that virtue of vigilance.

That is the second question, *What is the* diakonia *of the deacon?* I think we have to be prepared to give a very clear answer to people who ask.

The third question flows from the first two. What is the relationship of the diaconate to the lay faithful? How does the diaconate work to activate the laity in their specific role in the church and in the world? Now this is going to be a very difficult thing to explain and to live out. I don't know how many times I hear people refer to "lay deacons." There is no such thing. But they have that sense of confusion. As the *Directory* points out, following again the *Directory from Rome,* permanent deacons are in an especially advantageous place, that is to bring the work of the church to the world around us and to activate the laity. The vast majority of deacons are *not* full-time members of the church organization. The majority of deacons work at a profession in the world. It is specifically *because* they are part of this world, but yet a *sacrament* of Christ in his body the church, that they are in this powerful position of demonstrating to the laity how specifically the vocation to holiness can be pursued and can be achieved in the very work in the world that they do.

I am *not* suggesting that deacons become street corner preachers. I *am* suggesting that simply by the way that a deacon lives, by the way he speaks, and by the way he relates to other people, he is going to manifest the power of the gospel and become one of the most effective evangelizers.

I know I've told some of you the story of what happened to me as a young college student. One summer I worked in my father's factory. I worked in the warehouse. And the language among these workers was not exactly Shakespearian. There was a fellow worker who was a Pentecostal and wore his religion on his sleeve. He was the object of merciless comments and attacks. One day he asked if he could eat lunch with me. I said sure, of course looking over my shoulder to the other workers who wondered if I had converted. We were eating lunch and all of a sudden he said, "You're a Christian aren't you?" I said, "Well, yeah, I'm a Christian. How did you know?" He said, "We've been here together working for a month and a half and I have never heard you use a curse word, a swear word, or a vulgar expression." I first thought to myself, *If I did my father would whack me at home!* I then thought to myself, *Why am I not identifying more with this man, rather than hanging back?* It was what the charismatics call "being convicted." I think a deacon is in that position to really call the laity to the transformation of the world according to the pattern of Christ. It is important then for the laity to see this deacon, who during the week they may see down the hall working, to then see him on the altar, because, in a way, this makes sacramental that call to holiness.

Another way by which I think a deacon can do this is through the living out of another sacrament he has celebrated and continues to celebrate, namely marriage. I have often said that one of the greatest gifts that our church can give to the world today is a firm example of married and family life. This is one of those particular challenges that we are going to have to address. The *Directory* does it to a certain extent. But I don't think we have very thoroughly thought out the consequences of the effect of sacramental ordination on the already existing sacrament of marriage. Here a deacon is called to the *diakonia* of Christ, which is the full giving of one's self to the life of Christ and his ministry. In the sacrament of marriage he has been called to do this for a particular person, his wife. How do the two fit together? This is going to take some work, both theological reflection and sociological investigation.

I remember talking to a teenage son of one of the deacons, who said it was all right his father was a deacon as long as he did not preach in their own parish because he didn't want to become a preacher's kid. There are these kinds of challenges. In the formation process there has to be attention paid to the stability of the marriage. I had an experience with a divorce on the part of a deacon and his wife. It was devastating to the parish. They started taking sides. And here the deacon is supposed to be an instrument of communion. I just mention that because I think it is something we are going to have to address before we address the particular form or shape of a formation program.

As you may know, the *Directory* has three actual documents in it. The first is the actual *Directory* that is the norm for the dioceses in the United States. The other two are suggested documents to be used for implementation. It is an important document to read.

I thank you for this opportunity to talk to you about the *New National Directory.* I hope that I've drawn you into the document.

Implementation Strategies for the *New National Directory of Deacons*

Deacon William T. Ditewig, PhD
Executive Director
Secretariat for the Diaconate
United States Conference of Catholic Bishops

With the December 2004 promulgation of the *National Directory for the Formation, Ministry and Life of Permanent Deacons in the United States,* the Catholic Church in the United States has moved into a new phase in the development of the diaconate. This document, when seen in context, reflects the growing maturation of the renewed diaconate flowing out from more than thirty-five years of pastoral experience as well as the impact of recent documents from the Holy See. In today's presentation, I hope to do three things. First, I want to offer a brief historical sketch of the role of the United States Conference of Catholic Bishops [herein USCCB] in the development of the diaconate in the United States. The *National Directory* is, after all, a document of *our* episcopal conference and issued under its authority. It is therefore necessary to understand something of its nature and responsibility. Second, we will review the development of the *National Directory*. The promulgation of the document was the result of a dynamic process, and the process itself is illuminating and helpful in interpreting the text. Third, and finally, I will offer six suggested elements for the implementation of the *National Directory*. This list is simply suggestive, not exhaustive.

Part One: The USCCB and the Diaconate

Not surprisingly, the specific responsibility of episcopal conferences for the diaconate finds its source in the Second Vatican Council. The Dogmatic Constitution on the Church *(Lumen gentium)* paragraph 29 says simply, "It pertains to the competent territorial bodies of bishops, of one kind or another, with the approval of the Supreme Pontiff, to decide whether and where it is opportune for such deacons to be established for the care of souls."[1] On June 18, 1967, Pope Paul VI implemented this conciliar decision through *Sacrum Diaconatus Ordinem*. In establishing the first norms for the renewal of the diaconate, Pope Paul picked up on this responsibility, writing, "It is the task of the legitimate assemblies of bishops of episcopal conferences to discuss, with the consent of the Supreme Pontiff whether and where—in view of the good of the faithful—the diaconate is to be instituted as a proper and permanent rank of the hierarchy."[2] This national responsibility for the renewal of the diaconate is something that the bishops of the United States have taken quite seriously. Since 1967 the bishops have maintained a continuous structural element dedicated to the diaconate. This has not been the practice in other parts of the world. I believe that this constant and consistent dedication to the diaconate by the Conference is one of the reasons that the diaconate has flourished as it has in this country.

Immediately after Pope Paul promulgated those first norms, five episcopal conferences requested and received authority to ordain permanent deacons: Germany, France, Italy, Brazil, and Cameroon. These countries had been discussing the possibilities of a renewed diaconate for many years and were ready and eager for the diaconate.[3] After receiving the approval of the Holy See, these countries moved immediately into preparations for ordination, with the first ordinations being celebrated in 1968 in Germany and Cameroon.[4]

I want to focus briefly on the first of these ordination classes. On April 28, 1968, five men were ordained deacons for Cologne, Germany. They ranged in age from thirty-five to forty-seven, and had been in formal preparation for eight years. With the appearance of the first "Deacon Circle" in 1951 in Freiburg, Germany, many men had pursued formation on the remote possibility of eventual ordination at some point in the future. In the case of these men, they began formation in 1960: before the Council had even begun, before the decision was made to renew the diaconate was made, and before Paul VI implemented that decision. In addition to being a marvelous act of faith and service, it is also interesting to note that this means they began formation when they were aged twenty-seven to thirty-nine. All of these men were still working in secular occupations (although one was a full-time diocesan official) and were married with families. I point this out because a current issue in the diaconate in this country is the aging of the diaconate, where the average age of deacons is now at least sixty-one, and the average age at ordination is now around fifty-five. Everywhere else in the world, especially in Europe, the average age of deacons remains about forty-one. This is not the time or the place to address this issue, but certainly bishops and directors of diaconate formation programs need to consider the age of applicants closely. It also underscores a point made quite pointedly in the *National Directory:* that formation for the diaconate should involve the entire family as appropriate. This is how formation is handled in many parts of Europe: the entire family comes to formation, with teams of qualified youth ministers caring for the children while their parents are in class; during meals and prayer times, however, the families are together. Several United States dioceses are now following this same approach, allowing younger families the opportunity to participate in formation.

While the diaconate in Europe and Africa was moving ahead smartly in 1967 and 1968, here in the United States our Conference moved a bit more deliberately. Since there had not been the same level of theological and pastoral discussion here about the possibilities of the diaconate, when our bishops gathered in 1967 they discussed Pope Paul's document. Based on this conversation, they commissioned a research study to be done by the Catholic Theological Society of America (CTSA) on what a renewed diaconate might contribute to pastoral life in the United States. They also appointed a new *ad hoc* Committee on the Permanent Diaconate to oversee this whole process. In 1968, the CTSA completed their report and recommended to the Committee that the Conference should move forward with a request to the Holy See to renew the diaconate in the United States. The full body of bishops agreed, and the letter to the Holy See was prepared and submitted in April 1968. The Holy See quickly granted permission in August 1968. Therefore, at the November 1968 General Meeting of the full body of bishops, they approved the transition of the *ad hoc* Committee on the Permanent Diaconate to the status of a standing (permanent) Committee, with a supporting Secretariat, and this structure has been in place ever since. At this point, the Conference did something else of great significance: the full body of bishops approved the first four training centers for diaconate formation: two national sites and two diocesan sites. Two things are significant in this regard: First, many dioceses and institutions are exploring again the possibility of regional models for formation (in addition to diocesan models), and some insights can be gained from these early national projects. Second, the pattern was established whereby the episcopal conference was the approval authority for each and every formation program established in the United States.

The first permanent deacon ordained in the United States was Michael Cole, ordained on June 1, 1969, by Archbishop Fulton J. Sheen in Rochester, New York. Deacon Cole was a former Episcopalian priest who had recently been received into the church. It was determined that since he already had extensive theological and pastoral experience, no additional formation was necessary. Unfortunately, the year following his ordination he resumed his former ministry in the Anglican communion and assumed a pastorate in Canada. The next permanent deacon ordained in the United States was Paul McCardle in Kansas City-St. Joseph. He was ordained on May 24, 1970, by Bishop Charles Helmsing. Deacon Paul became the first deacon ordained following a period of formation designed for him.

In 1971 the first large classes of deacons were ordained in several dioceses. It was also in 1971 that the Bishops' Committee on the Diaconate issued its first guidelines on formation. When the *Code of Canon Law* was revised in 1983, new canons related to the diaconate needed to be reflected in diaconate formation. Specifically related to the topic at hand—the responsibility of the episcopal conferences for the renewal of the diaconate—c. 236 directed that:

> According to the prescripts of the *conference of bishops,* those aspiring to the permanent diaconate are to be formed to nourish a spiritual life

and instructed to fulfill correctly the duties proper to that order....Men of a more mature age, whether celibate or married, are to spend three years in a program defined by the *conference of bishops.*

Once again, it is to be the various episcopal conferences that set the standards for formation, and the Conference issued new formation guidelines in 1984.

In addition to setting formation standards, the USCCB, as seen above, also approved each new diaconate formation program established throughout the country. However, with the massive explosion of new programs throughout the 1970s, that task soon became impossible to administer. As a result, programs started springing up everywhere with no approval from the Bishops' Conference. In those salad days the Executive Director of the Secretariat for the Diaconate would gather informally with the directors of formation programs to discuss formation issues. However, as the number of formation programs grew, this became impractical, and the National Association of Diaconate Directors was formed in 1976. Officially, USCCB approval of diaconate formation programs was required until the promulgation of the new *National Directory* in December 2004. What is now strongly recommended, however, is that whenever a diocese initiates diaconate formation or significantly changes an existing program, a formal evaluation be requested by the Bishops' Committee on the Diaconate [BCD].

Implementation Strategies

Paragraph 296 of the *National Directory* outlines the current responsibilities of the USCCB; specifically, the responsibilities of the Bishops' Committee on the Diaconate and the Secretariat for the Diaconate. Six particular areas are identified: (1) provide information on the diaconate to the bishops of the United States; (2) establish national norms for the selection, formation, placement, ministry, life of aspirants, candidates, and deacons; (3) provide formal evaluation of formation programs; (4) initiate resources for a "structured catechesis" on the diaconate; (5) initiate national studies of the diaconate; and, (6) maintain a current statistical database on deacons in the United States. In the past, these items were handled directly by the Secretariat. However, given the vast growth of the diaconate many of these issues, such as national studies or the maintenance of a national statistical database, are now directed by the USCCB but carried out by professional research organizations such as the Center for Applied Research in the Apostolate (CARA) at Georgetown University.

Paragraph 297 describes the relationship of the Bishops' Committee on the Diaconate and the various national associations related to the diaconate. Specifically, "at the invitation of the Bishops' Committee on the Diaconate, the executive officers of the national associations serve as advisors to the Committee." This advisory role "promotes the accountability of each association to the Committee....In addition, these associations bring unique perspectives to the Committee's deliberations."

In summary, from the very beginning of the renewed diaconate at the Second Vatican Council, it has been the responsibility of the various Conferences of bishops to oversee and provide the overall leadership for the development of the diaconate in the United States.

Part Two: The Development of the *National Directory*

Three principal factors precipitated the development of the new *National Directory*. First, the pastoral experience gained since the 1984 Guidelines had significantly dated them; revisions were clearly in order. Second, the nature of pastoral ministry in the United States had grown increasingly complex, with a growing shortage of priests and expanding involvement of lay ecclesial ministers; these realities required an even more sophisticated understanding of the nature and mission of the diaconate itself. Third, the Holy See had become even more involved in the renewal of the diaconate, and it is on this third point that I wish to offer a few observations, due to their significant influence on the development and content of the *National Directory*.

In 1995, the Congregation for Catholic Education and the Congregation for Clergy promulgated two documents on the formation, ministry, and life of presbyters. Upon their release, these two dicasteries announced that similar documents would be developed on the diaconate. On February 22, 1998, the *Basic Norms for the Formation of Permanent*

Deacons and the *Directory for the Ministry and Life of Permanent Deacons* were promulgated jointly by these Congregations, along with a Joint Introduction.

The *Basic Norms* were issued by the Congregation for Catholic Education, and it asserts a strong level of authority, declaring that it is a directive and not merely a guideline. Furthermore, episcopal conferences are to use this document in the preparation of their own norms for formation. The *Directory* was promulgated by the Congregation for the Clergy, and it refers to itself as a "general executory decree." In both cases, the Holy See is clear: these texts are not merely advisory; they are *directives* to be followed by Conferences of Bishops preparing their own norms for the formation, ministry, and life of deacons. If one closely examines the endnotes of the *National Directory,* it is easy to see just how significantly these two texts have influenced our own.

The production of the *Directory* involved dozens of bishops, many more dozens of deacons, wives of deacons, priests, and laypersons over seven years and at least seven drafts. It spanned three committees of bishops. Considerable consultation was done with many groups of experts in many fields and with a variety of agencies and associations, especially the NADD. The full body of bishops reviewed the entire document on several occasions, and it was reviewed twice by a number of dicasteries of the Holy See. It would be hard to envision a document being given more care and scrutiny in its preparation.

Once the actual work began on the preparation of the document, an important consideration by the bishops was the juridical and magisterial character their own document should possess. Whereas previous United States documents had been "Guidelines," the new document required a stronger character, especially given the nature of the Vatican documents themselves. Since the Second Vatican Council, a new genre of ecclesiastical document has developed known as a "directory." A *directory* is a document comprehensive in scope that provides foundational theological and theoretical bases for extensive principles to be used in the development and implementation of a pastoral concern. Directories may also contain specific application of current law and convey new particular law. The intent of a directory is to offer a common vision without imposing rigid uniformity. The *National Directory*, therefore, is intended as a document that implements many of the universal principles found in the documents from the Holy See while at the same time offering its own principles for further implementation at regional and diocesan levels. Most people are familiar with documents such as the *General Directory for Catechesis* and its United States counterpart, the newly promulgated *National Directory for Catechesis*. One may also point to directories on ecumenism, liturgy, the pastoral ministry of bishops, and now, on the diaconate.

As may be inferred from this observation about the nature of a directory, one must always keep in mind the sheer scope involved with the *National Directory*. This document covers much more than the formational aspects of preparing candidates for possible ordination. It attempts to situate (however briefly) the diaconate itself within its broader sacramental and ministerial context in the life of the church. I wish to stress this point, since it may seem tempting simply to turn to those chapters dealing with the details of formation. To do so without first internalizing the foundational sections on the theology, spirituality, and ministry of the deacon would be a grave mistake. The formational sections of the document are grounded deeply within those foundational sections and should not be considered apart from them.

In short, what authority do the bishops of the United States give to this document? Paragraph 14 states, "This *Directory* is prescribed for the use of the diocesan bishop, as well as those responsible for its implementation. The specifications published in this *Directory* are to be incorporated by each diocese of the Conference...." Paragraph 15 addresses the objective and interpretation of the document, stating clearly that "this Directory is normative throughout the United States Conference of Catholic Bishops and its territorial sees....[It] will guide and harmonize the formation programs drawn up by each diocese of the Conference that 'at times vary greatly from one to another.'"

Part Three: Six Elements for Implementation

I want to conclude by offering six essential elements to consider when beginning to implement the *National*

Directory in your dioceses and archdioceses. There could undoubtedly be many more; these are offered merely as suggestions to spark additional thought and creativity. These six components involve interpretation, context, scope, content, attitude, and resources.

1. Interpretation: "By Bishops, for Bishops"

In my opinion, one the most critical things to understand about this document is that it was written *by* bishops *for* bishops. Time and time again during the drafting process, the bishops would mention this fact. They were constantly concerned that the document say precisely what they felt their brother bishops needed to read about the diaconate. This means that this text was *not* prepared primarily for the deacons or priests of the country; the principal audience is the college of bishops, and those who assist the bishops in carrying out the norms of the document. This fact should be borne in mind whenever reading or studying the text. If there is an overarching theme of the *Directory* it is to stress the sacramental relationship that binds the deacon in a special way to the apostolic ministry of the bishop himself, flowing from sacred ordination into the ministry and life of Christ. I am asking all of you as deacon directors to promise this hermeneutic and theme are the foundation for everything that follows.

2. *Context: Link between Relationships and Structures*

This sacramental relationship between the bishop and his deacons provides the context for the integration of the order of deacons into the pastoral life of the diocesan church. Consider first the theological basis of chapter 1, grounded as it is in an ecclesiology of *communio*. The *Directory* moves directly from this presentation into the ministry and life of deacons in chapter 2, offering twenty-one paragraphs on the relationships of deacons that are brought about by ordination, beginning with several very strong paragraphs on the relationship with the bishop. For example, paragraph 41 says:

> The deacon exercises his ministry within a specific pastoral context—the communion and mission of a diocesan Church. He is in *direct relationship* with the diocesan bishop with whom he is in communion and under whose authority he exercises his ministry....It is therefore a *particular responsibility* of the bishop to provide for the pastoral care of the deacons of his diocese. The bishop discharges this responsibility *both* personally and through the director of deacon personnel. *(Emphasis added)*

Given the fact that bishops in this document are addressing their brother bishops, this is particularly strong.

In chapter 8, paragraph 257, notice the linkage between the role of the bishop and the role of the deacon in an overall pastoral plan for ministry in the diocese.

> The establishment or renewal of diaconal ministry within a diocesan Church needs to be conceived and established *within an overall diocesan plan for ministry* in which the diaconate is seen as an *integral component* in addressing pastoral needs. In this way, deacons, who are ordained for service to the *diocesan Church,* will have a richer and firmer sense of their identity and purpose, as will those who collaborate in ministry with them. *(Emphasis added)*

Many dioceses *still* do not have a pastoral plan for ministry: perhaps this is a particular service in which deacons might provide leadership. Certainly, the bishops are reminding themselves that deacons are a critical component of whatever pastoral planning is necessary. I would also point out that in the last national study on the diaconate, reported in 1996, one of the major concerns that surfaced was that deacons were being wonderfully received as parish ministers, but that people were not yet recognizing the fact that deacons are ordained for service to the *entire* diocesan church. It is clear in the *Directory* that the bishops want there to be no confusion on this issue: deacons serve him in the whole diocesan church.

3. Scope: Diocesan Church

This theme of service to the entire diocesan church and the communities in which that church finds itself provides the scope of the document itself. I mentioned above that chapter 2 offers twenty-one paragraphs on the various relationships effected by the sacrament of Orders. The categories discussed sketch out the ecclesial breadth of the *Directory*. Paragraphs 41–47 address the relationship with and responsibilities of the diocesan bishop. Paragraphs 48–49 refer to the diocesan church in general; 50–53, diocesan presbyters; 55, the religious in the diocese; 56–57, the laity; 54, those men in formation for possible ordination; 58–60, society at large. Finally, paragraph 61 highlights an essential unity in all pastoral activity, and the deacon is involved in all of it.

You will notice that I have not mentioned some of the most important relationships of all for deacons, especially those who are married; namely, his relationships with his wife and family. These relationships are certainly addressed, and at some length, in the text. What I am highlighting here, however, is the scope of relationships brought about by the act of ordination itself. This is not meant to minimize other sacramental relationships, but to see all of them in context.

4. Content: Current Process, Law, Policy

As you begin to implement the *Directory*, it is important to know and appreciate what you are already doing. Keep in mind that when the Holy See began its work on the two documents released in 1998, they were heavily influenced, in a quite positive way, with the experience of the United States church with the diaconate. So, do not be hasty in feeling you must start from scratch! Nonetheless, your evaluation of your current formation program and processes must be honest, thorough, and comprehensive. The key here will be to integrate the strengths of your existing experience into whatever modifications you and your bishop decide to make. Furthermore, you should find ways to even more systematically integrate the diaconate into the various pastoral structures of your diocesan church in light of the *Directory*. For example, what policies exist in your diocese regarding those persons who might be assigned to provide pastoral leadership to parishes in the absence of a priest (c. 517.2)? This issue is addressed within the *Directory* and so existing diocesan policy needs to be reexamined. Similar reviews may involve the incorporation of deacons into diocesan liability insurance coverage and so on.

Some possible points to assist you in getting started would include: the norms provided at the end of chapters 2 through 8, the particular law provided in chapter 2; chapter 8 and its discussion of existing diocesan structures; and, finally, the "secondary document" provided at the end of the book, which offers you a self-evaluation instrument that may be used to great benefit. You will find that some of what you are already doing is fine as it is, while you will also find areas in need of great reform. This systematic review process, however, will give you a valuable template with which to operate.

5. *Attitude: Creativity, Continuity, Consistency*

As we all know, the attitude with which one approaches a task can have great influence on the results of that task. I am suggesting that our attitude with regard to implementing the *Directory* ought to be, "We are going to implement this document fully and completely." In other words, we should not lightly assume that certain parts of the document do not apply to us, because they do!

A measure of diocesan adaptability may be seen in the notion of "basic standards for formation" in the first place. When approaching the notion of diaconal formation, the bishops *could* have simply directed, for example, that all deacon candidates obtain a college degree; they deliberately chose not to do so. They *could* have designed a national curriculum to be implemented throughout the country; they deliberately chose not to do so. They *could* have said simply that each diocesan bishop should design his own formation programs using their own formation standards; they deliberately chose not to do so. What the bishops *did* do was develop a set of national standards to be used by every diocese, while leaving specific curriculum design, development, and assessment to each diocese. With this in mind, have an attitude of creativity, continuity, and consistency.

a. Creativity

Your creativity will be stretched as you consider, for example, how "assessment" will be constructed and implemented throughout your formation program. How will the "basic standards" be adapted? Notice, if a basic standard seems, on first reading, not to be applicable to your diocese, I suggest you reread it with a view to finding out how it *does* apply. Remember, the "standards" are to be implemented and adapted as necessary, but *not* ignored or disregarded. Finally, what resources are available to you? Think outside the box; traditional resources may or may not be available: schools, institutes, and so on. However, what other resources *are* also available, such as high technology? What can be used to help design and "deliver" the formation experience to candidates in your diocese?

b. Continuity

Here are the questions resulting from your diocesan self-assessment. What components of your current formation program and current diocesan structures may be continued as they are, or with only modest adaptation? And for those changes that are necessary, how will they be transitioned into existing structures, curriculum, and policies?

c. Consistency

How does diaconate formation relate to other ministry formation programs in the diocese? How might they be integrated (or not)? How may resources be shared? How is the formation program documented? If your staff were to leave suddenly, could it be replicated? Documentation of every aspect of the program is essential, not only for accurate record keeping, but so that it can also be shared with others. Finally, documentation is critical because of the need for greater transportability of diaconal formation programs. Deacons, and deacon candidates, tend to be quite mobile since they are frequently moved by their employers. This has been a particular challenge in the past, and the bishops are hopeful that the challenges presented by deacons and candidates moving from one diocese to another will be minimized by a consistent, well-documented application of the basic standards across the country.

6. Resources

This last element speaks to the need to look beyond "deacon-specific" resources in the formation of deacons. For example, who else is doing similar work in formation? One example: We are here in April [2005] in New Orleans discussing the implementation of the *National Directory,* including the "basic standards for formation." How many here are going to return in June [2005] to New Orleans? "Why?" you may ask. Because the National Association of Lay Ministry (NALM) is holding their own annual conference here, and they are going to be addressing the theme, "Raising the Bar: Applying the National Standards." In other words, the

NALM is embarked on a very similar project as we are; we should be working in collaboration with them. Other resources that might be tapped include the National Organization for the Continuing Education of Roman Catholic Clergy (NOCERCC). This organization has for many years focused on the continuing formation of priests, but has in recent years realized that it has, by its very nature, a responsibility for continuing education of deacons as well. Still another resource is the USCCB itself. We have more than three hundred employees in our Washington headquarters who would be most happy to help you with specific aspects of diaconate formation: liturgy, social justice and peace, family, youth, pro-life activities, religious education, and catechesis: the list is almost endless. Finally, there are the many Catholic colleges, research universities, and institutes who are often looking for opportunities for collaboration.

The message of this component is simple enough: We must always look beyond the obvious resources and see how we might take advantage of all the expertise and experience that is out there just waiting to be tapped. This is also a great way to familiarize these other institutions and agencies with the nature and work of the diaconate itself; all can benefit from this mutual interaction.

Conclusion: USCCB and NADD in Partnership

The responsibility of the USCCB is clearly reflected in the *National Directory*. The Committee on the Diaconate and our offices exist to provide guidance, direction, a sense of unity, and doctrinal understanding with regard to the diaconate. The specific details of implementation remain to be worked out locally while respecting what is in the *Directory*. The way the bishops expect your programs to be implemented and evaluated is by making use of their service of providing formal evaluations, a process that is clearly spelled out in the *Directory*.

From my perspective as the Executive Director of the Secretariat for the Diaconate at the USCCB, the role of the NADD in this process is one of leadership *and* collaboration. The NADD can collect, collate, and publish the numerous "best practices" available from all of your member dioceses. In collaboration and dialogue with the BCD, the NADD serves as advisors and mentors to the bishops, offering insights gained from national involvement in diaconal formation.

In looking to the future, it is good to remember that the official *recognitio* given by the Holy See to the *Directory* is a mere five years. Although this has become standard practice, it still means that we must already be looking ahead to what will happen at that point in time. The bishops may, of course, request an extension of the *recognitio* beyond the five-year mark; but it is prudent to anticipate that the bishops will not do so or, even if they did, that the Holy See may not grant the request. In that case, we must be prepared to revise or completely rewrite the document for a new approval process. In this regard, I ask that you begin now with a critical examination of the document as you begin its implementation. Stay in touch with me about things you find in need of adjustment or correction or revision; if we do this as we go along, future revisions need not be as wrenching as this last process turned out to be.

It is in the NADD that wisdom and experience come together in a most unique way. Regardless of what the future holds, the NADD will continue to be a key player in the ongoing development of the renewed diaconate in the United States.

Notes

1. *Lumen gentium* 29.

2. Paul VI, *motu proprio Sacrum Diaconatus Ordinem* (June 18, 1967), I/1.

3. One author points to an 1840 exchange of letters between a physician and a priest-friend in Germany as an early indicator of the interest being expressed there and elsewhere in Europe.

4. April 28, 1968, Cologne, Germany; November 3, 1968, Rottenburg, Germany; December 8, 1968, Bamburg, Germany; December 8, 1968, Douala, Cameroon.

Responses to the
Keynotes

Response to Archbishop Hughes: An Experience of Restorative Justice

Michael Kennedy

Pastor of Dolores Mission, Los Angeles

On October 12, 2005, I participated in a press conference on the Adultification of the Justice System and, particularly, on the sentencing of children to life without parole. Two youth spoke about how they were given another opportunity and why it's important not to look at incarcerated youth as monsters.

Our country's overreliance on punishment results in over 2,200 children serving life sentence without the possibility of parole. Other countries combined have a total of twelve offenders serving the same sentence. Our country's fear and preoccupation with crime is overwhelming. Sadly, we project this on those in the criminal justice system. There is an alternative to this, however.

Rita Chairez, a community organizer at Dolores Mission Church, in Los Angeles, was with me on the day of the conference. On the way back from the event, Rita was trembling after being in touch with so many bad feelings. She shared how the fifth anniversary of the death of her brother Robert is coming up. Robert was killed in a drive-by shooting one balmy evening as he sat on his porch. Rita described how hard it is for her to think that one of the young men who spoke at the conference could have killed her brother, and mentioned that she didn't even want to think about celebrating Robert's anniversary.

As I rode back to the church, I thought of when I was phoned to go bless Robert's body at General Hospital, in Los Angeles. In spite of the sadness and pain, I never saw hate take over the hearts of anyone in Rita's family. At a recent conference at Dolores Mission Church, some victims of violence expressed their hate toward others who had harmed their families. Rita's own conscious choice to forgive, however, has led her and her family in a different direction, where hope and life abound.

I remember how, right after Robert was killed, I invited Rita to speak at a Sunday Mass at Central Juvenile Hall, where two hundred minors were present. Rita spoke of the impact of Robert's violent death on her family. Some of the minors were moved and wrote moving letters when I met with them the week after. One of these young men wrote, "Señora Chairez, I am sad about what happened to your brother. I know what you feel like. My brother was killed when I was eight. When I listened to you, I understood much better what my mother went through the day my brother was killed. You made me think of what I am doing and how I would like to change. I am sorry for what happened."

Rita had her pain acknowledged. She received an apology, and in some way felt vindicated. The young men at Juvenile Hall understood more clearly how crime affects everyone, and they took responsibility for their actions. Furthermore, they empathized with Rita, finding common ground to listen to and discuss her story.

The experience between Rita and the youth is one of *restorative justice*—understanding that victim and offender are interconnected, can listen to each other, and repair any injuries caused by violence. The process begins by honoring the fundamental dignity of every individual and creating right relationships among victims, offenders, and communities. Rita and the youth were able to enter into a process of healing each other.

Yesterday was the fifth year anniversary of Robert's death. Rita's family took another step toward healing by attending one of our Sunday liturgies and praying for healing. What of the pain and hurt caused by Robert's death? It's still there, though the injuries are not as painful. Rita's family has embraced a justice that is restorative. Their restoration is for us, at Dolores Mission Church, a sign of hope for victims and offenders.

At Dolores Mission, we have seen youth of fifteen years of age sentenced to life behind bars, families devastated by killings, and, at the same time, individuals who work to change unjust laws and minister to the incarcerated. Rita is a symbol of all of all the above. Her vision, hope, and leadership are examples of how to restore people from their pain and brokenness.

Response to Bishop Campbell: The Impact of the *New National Directory*

Deacon Owen F. Cummings

Regents' Professor of Theology
Mount Angel Seminary

I

At the personal and experiential level, I began my studies for the permanent diaconate exactly twenty years ago in 1985, and was ordained in 1989. When our course of studies began, we had the great good fortune of being in a diocese with its own major seminary. That meant that we had access to well-trained theologians of high caliber for the duration of the course. This was a blessing. There were seven of us altogether: an elementary school teacher, a high school teacher, two accountants, an attorney, a physician, and me, a theologian. Indeed, an interesting mix! The formation we received was academic and spiritual, but no less important, it was *participatory*. We helped in our constant interactions when we were together to shape each other; it was a real exercise in communion, in becoming more obviously one in Christ while being just as obviously different.

However, an acknowledged deficit during the period of formation was the paucity of credible theological literature and developed and directive guidelines from the Magisterium on the diaconate. As well as being formed theologically/academically, spiritually and pastorally, there was also this area of formation *as* deacons. It was in this particular area that there were few really persuasive resources. It would be fair to say that between 1985 and 1989 three books provided insight into the theology of the diaconate. First was Edward P. Echlin, *The Deacon in the Church: Past and Future* (Staten Island, NY: Alba House, 1971). It offered and continues to offer real help and insight. At the time, Echlin was a Jesuit priest teaching theology at John Carroll University in Cleveland. He had already published an article on the diaconate in the *American Ecclesiastical Review*.[1] Echlin is an accomplished theologian with an interest in liturgical and ecumenical theology, his first book being *The Anglican Eucharist in Ecumenical Perspective*.[2] He had also been chairman of the special committee of the Catholic Theological Society of America on the Permanent Diaconate. He was well placed to write on the diaconate, and his book did not and does not disappoint. It provides theological reflection on the diaconate out of careful attention to its historical development. Second was the Anglican theologian James M. Barnett's *The Diaconate, A Full and Equal Order.*[3] The book has gone through a revised edition, but originally it represented the substance of Barnett's work for the D.Min. at the University of the South, Sewanee. The first part of the book was largely historical, but the second part, running to almost one hundred pages, attempted with some success to reach out into the important areas of theology (especially ecclesiology) and formation. It was the most substantial work in English to date on the diaconate, and provided an excellent bibliography for others to go further. Third was the Collegeville Benedictine Michael Kwatera's *The Liturgical Ministry of Deacons.*[4] As the title suggests, Fr. Kwatera's book dealt solely with the liturgical role of the deacon and was of immense help to many. There was little else both available and accessible to deacons at the time.

The situation today has changed in great measure. There is a growing number of books on the diaconate, and foremost in this country in their promotion has been Paulist Press[5] and especially one of its editors, Kevin Carizzo DiCamillo. The time is now very ripe for more in-depth and wide-ranging theological work on the diaconate. The permanent diaconate is now, at least on the paper of *Lumen gentium* 29, some forty years old. Life begins at forty! Experience and reflection on experience has placed us all in a much better to place to think through diaconal theology. As well as this, there exist now *Basic Norms for the Formation of Permanent Deacons* from the Congregation for Catholic Education, and the *Directory for the Ministry and Life of Permanent Deacons* from the

Congregation for the Clergy. Both documents were published in 1998, and in 2005 they have been consolidated into the very fine *National Directory for the Formation, Ministry and Life of Permanent Deacons in the United States*.[6] One might also wish to add *From the Diakonia of Christ to the Diakonia of the Apostles* that has come recently from the International Theological Commission.[7] The national situation and, therefore, the local diocesan situation is now much better placed to engage with the diaconate.

II

Here in this present book, Bishop Frederick Campbell's fine essay is entitled "The Impact of the *New National Directory for the Formation, Ministry and Life of Permanent Deacons in the United States*." In this essay Bishop Campbell describes the impact of the *National Directory* both from his perspective of responsibility at the level of the National Conference of Catholic Bishops, but also as one who has had a hand in diaconal formation for many years. His essay is not intended to be a detailed exegesis of the many issues that are unfolded in the *Directory*, but rather to paint a large canvas of the most substantive issues raised. What now follows is commentary on the essay, commentary designed to point up areas of agreement and to seek further elucidation, and then suggestions for further theological reflection and development.

Bishop Campbell's essay is divided into two parts. The first part speaks of three general impacts of the *Directory:*

1. As an instrument to initiate or to evaluate a program of diaconal formation
2. As a blueprint for formation and ministry
3. As a tool in admission, discernment, and formation.

The second part is given over to a consideration of three questions:

1. What is a deacon?
2. What precisely is the service of *diakonia?*
3. What is the relationship of the diaconate to the laity?

As he introduces his essay and looks back, Bishop Campbell writes of his work with the diaconate beginning in 1978: "I suspect we did not know what we were doing...." I know what Bishop Campbell means. There was a *sense* of what was being done, a kind of intuitive *modus operandi,* but no theological or formational blueprint, as it were. Though Bishop Campbell does not explicitly advert to this in so many words, there was also in these earlier times of diaconal formation a powerful excitement and enthusiasm that something new was taking place, that the Holy Spirit was at work calling forth this restored ministry in the church. It would be unfortunate now that we have greater and more informed resources if this real experience of excitement got lost or marginalized. Now let us turn our attention to the three general impacts of the *National Directory.*

III

The immediate impact of the *National Directory*, according to Bishop Campbell, will lie in its helpfulness to bishops either in initiating a new program or in evaluating an existing program in diaconal formation. This is right on target. Each chapter of the *Directory*, as well as its secondary documents, will not only assist individual bishops in this regard, but will also draw the entire country into a more united, more integrated pedagogy for the diaconate. My suspicion is that Bishop Campbell is speaking here primarily though not exclusively of pre-ordination formation. However, there is more to be said, and this is what the bishop is moving toward in the next "impact."

Bishop Campbell moves on to comment on the impact of the *Directory* as "a blueprint for [deacons'] life in ministry." He is talking about what happens after ordination, and he admits in the early days to having some concerns about some deacons being licensed to preach because of weaknesses in their understanding of holy scripture. With the best will in the world, and even with the best resources in the world, no formational program for ministry in the church can be complete. Ineluctably there will be gaps in formation that can only be noticed and attended to through the actual experience of being a deacon. The same is true of seminary formation. When a seminarian is ordained a priest, it is true that he has behind him four years of theology (not to mention the now required thirty hours of philosophy!) in all its various dimensions, and a graduated induction into pastoral experience. No seminary professor, however, would characterize such a formation process as now complete with ordination. Yes, the young priest is ready to move forward, but he still requires the apprenticeship of an established priest-mentor, as well as ongoing formation in theology and spirituality. There is a shortage of adequate personnel to take an initiative in this respect for newly ordained priests, personnel who can continue the seminary nurture but in a different way. Nothing like a hothouse atmosphere is intended by these remarks, but rather the observation that new physicians (or new attorneys, or new therapists) also need monitoring and assistance and updating if the self-correcting process of learning is to take root and make for the flourishing of others. If, due to personnel challenges, bishops find this difficult to achieve satisfactorily, how much more challenging in a way is the ongoing formation of newly ordained deacons. They too require mentors whose established competence in theology, pastoral practice, homiletics, and spirituality can continue to craft and mold them. Post-ordination formation of deacons is every bit as important as pre-ordination formation. One of the eight chapters in the *National Directory* is concerned with post-ordination formation. In that chapter we read, "Ongoing formation must include and harmonize all the dimensions of the life and ministry of the deacon. Thus…it should be complete, systematic and personalized in its diverse aspects whether human, spiritual, intellectual or pastoral."[8] In paragraph 248 the *Directory* repeats this with regard to intellectual formation in these words: "The intellectual dimension of post-ordination formation must be systematic and substantive, deepening the intellectual content initially studied during the candidate path of formation." In my judgment this is not taken with sufficient seriousness in general. More careful planning by those with an established competence in theology and related disciplines is necessary if this recommendation is to be more than ink on paper. And it will cost money. Yet, if we care about the diaconate and its witness and role in the church, the money has to be found, used wisely by prudent investment in ongoing theological formation. This could not be more urgent.

The final impact of the *Directory* to which Bishop Campbell draws attention touches on criteria for admission, the process of discernment, and the quality of formation. This goes hand in hand with his first impact and is self-evidently cogent.

IV

The first of Bishop Campbell's three questions rising out of the *Directory* is, "What is a deacon?" He rejects a response that is based on what a deacon *does,* and opts for a response, found mainly in the earlier chapter of the text, that focuses on the "sacramental reality of the deacon." This is the most persuasive way to go. Thus, a deacon is an ordained person, clergy, but one who is particularly conformed to Christ as an icon of service. The deacon's entire life is meant to be about service, a service at the altar that is commensurate with service at the "altar of the world."

The second question, "What precisely is the service of *diakonia?*" continues this line of thinking. His excellency dismisses an exclusive association of service as service to the poor and needy. Poverty and need go beyond physical poverty and deed. He points to Sts. Stephen and Philip in the Acts of the Apostles. With their other five companions—later called deacons by Bishop Irenaeus of Lyons, and so subsequently in the history of the church—these men are to relieve the burden of the apostles by attending to the "waiting on tables" (Acts 6). Following the line of John N. Collins, this "waiting tables" is not probably to be understood as *literal* waiting at tables, but ministering the word to the Greek-speaking widows.[9] Indeed, Bishop Campbell points this out himself as he characterizes Stephen as a preacher-martyr and Philip as an educator. The central point seems to be that there ought to be no narrow or insular construal of what *diakonia* or "service" means. The bishop rightly maintains that the question is, "How does the deacon manifest himself in the church?" and the answer is, "There are many ways in which this *diakonia* of Christ can be established." *Diakonia* has to do with building up the church so that the church may build up the world in the direction of greater and more intimate communion with God-in-Christ. There is no one, exclusive way in which this is to be done. The history of the church shows us deacons building up the church to build up the world in a variety of capacities, in accordance with the way God has gifted them and the discernment of their bishops.[10]

Further, a deacon is to be permanent. Paragraph 77 of the *Directory* underscores the permanency of the order by issuing a caveat about ordaining a permanent deacon who has been widowed or who is celibate. Failure to appreciate this point would seem to imply that in respect of the priesthood the diaconate is inferior, whereas the theology would seem to insist that in respect of the priesthood the diaconate is not *inferior* but *different*. The bishop rightly recognizes the need for catechesis on the diaconate.

Bishop Campbell's third question is this: "What is the relationship of the diaconate to the lay faithful?" It is a key question certainly, but, if it is such a central question, it needs to be expanded in the direction of *all* ordained ministry in the church. If deacons are ordained—that is, are *clergy*—then the question must not stop at the relationship of the diaconate to the lay faithful but must include all the faithful, including those who are ordained—deacons, priests, and bishops. What is the relationship of *all* the ordained—and, therefore, what is the relationship of deacons—to the lay faithful?

One habitual tendency in theology responding to this question is to focus on the past. The Lord Jesus is the source and foundation of all ministry in the church. Indeed, the Lord Jesus *is* the church, sacramentally rendered present in human beings who, before heaven, always have feet of clay. By focusing on the past, theologians look to ground the threefold shape of ministry in the church in the scriptures, seeing this threefold

shape instanced in and emergent from the Lord Jesus as represented especially in the Gospels. This approach might then go
on to look at the Pastoral Letters (1 and 2 Timothy and Titus)
as demonstrating, even if inchoately, the emergence of this ministry in New Testament times. Thus, we read about presbyter-
bishops in 1 Timothy 3:1–7. "In all likelihood those bishops
were presbyters; but since 5:17 indicates that only certain presbyters were involved in preaching and teaching, probably not
all presbyters were bishops. The claim that anyone who aspires
to the role of a bishop aspires to a noble function (3:1) shows
how highly the position was esteemed."[11] So, we know about
presbyters and bishops. The same letter in 3:8–13 proceeds to
speak of deacons alongside these presbyter-bishops. Their
credentials are not significantly different from those of the
presbyter-bishops, and we simply do not know what the functions of each order were at the time. But, at least we see the
beginnings of what will become the threefold order of ministry.
We could then move on to St. Ignatius of Antioch and to other
patristic texts that help us understand something further of this
ecclesially developing ministry. This is profoundly helpful in
trying to grasp how our Catholic shape of ministry grows and
is refined over time. Catholics live *on* the past. Tradition is the
living faith of that past. It is essential to do theology by looking to the past.

It is no less essential to do theology by looking to the
future. I mean by "the future" the Parousia, that point at which
in St. Paul's unsurpassed expression "God will be everything to
everyone" (1 Cor. 15:28). That is the *telos* or endpoint of all

creation, the final flourishing of all in God. That also is the purpose of the church. The Irish School of Ecumenics in Dublin has as its motto, *Floreat ut pereat:* "May it so flourish that it will not be necessary!" The school's commitment is to Christian unity, and so it prays and works that unity may come about so that the school will be redundant. Something similar is true of the church and ministry.

In *Lumen gentium* 1 we read, "The Church is a kind of sacrament or sign of intimate union with God and of the unity of all mankind." That conciliar passage is a paraphrase of the Parousia. The church exists as a sign of the Parousia, and, because a sign/sacrament in Catholic theology brings about that of which it is a sign, the church in being all that the church is, furthers or promotes this communion with God and with one another. We can never forget that this is what the church is all about, this the *raison d'être* of the church. Pope Benedict XVI puts it crisply when he says, "Talking about the church is talking about God and can be correct only in that sense."[12] Talking about the church is talking about God reaching out to draw us into the divine life. That's what we mean by the shorthand word *grace*. It is to enable the church to act in accord with its function that the ordained ministry exists. If the church is to be the harbinger of the Parousia, the sacrament of communion with God and with one another, if it is to look like and to promote creation as it will be at the end-time, the deacons, priests, and bishops exist to promote, to enable, to further this purpose of the church. The ordained ministry is thus not an end in itself but the divinely appointed means of furthering

God's own end for the church. If you like, ordained ministry exists to put itself out of business eschatologically! That is what is meant by "looking to the future." The restoration of the permanent diaconate is part of this charismatic, Spirit-led conciliar tradition that is both grounded in the past and looking to the future. The liturgical theologian Peter Fink, SJ, has put it well: "It is in function of the church's past, what we remember, and of the church's future, what we are summoned to become, that the ministry of the ordained has taken shape."[13]

The relationship of deacons to the lay faithful (and so in different ways and with different responsibilities the relationship of the presbyterate and of the episcopate to the lay faithful) is to do all they can do and what is episcopally asked of them, in part determined by our past and in part being called by the future that is God, both to invite and to enable the laity to live more fully into their divine baptismal vocation. It is to do all that they can do and are asked to do to further this communion with God for which the church exists. Deacons do this by serving as they can in accord with their giftedness and as they are asked. The faithful have a right to see the Parousial Christ in the ordained already at work, here and now, luring and attracting, persuading and enabling all of them, and so "all of each other," into greater and greater communion with the Divine Communion.

Perhaps the question, "What is the relationship of the diaconate to the lay faithful?" is sometimes hemmed around with a hermeneutic of suspicion so that it becomes, "Do we really need deacons, ordained men, to do what deacons do?

Couldn't the laity just do these things and get on with the business of being church alongside their priests and bishops? Is the diaconate not just another clericalist way of dominating the laity so that they are kept in an immature, infantile Christian state, and do not take initiatives for themselves?" This way of putting and understanding the question—a question as has been noted that may be put to *any* ordained minister—seems, at least in part, framed by a way of looking at reality as

> the "will to power," the bold assertion of self over and against nature and other selves....[This "will to power"] now largely determines our political, cultural, social, and even ecclesial conversations....When this Nietzscheanism—implicit or explicit—comes to shape our discussions of the relationship between ordained and nonordained, we are already lost.[14]

Being church, and *a fortiori* being a minister in the church, in our terms being a deacon, ought to have nothing to do with this "will to power." It is about seeing reality, especially the reality of human persons as self-donation so that God's holy name as Self-Donation may be more readily recognized and responded to. Donation is the name of creation, and self-donation is the rhythm of human creation. We refuse to see reality as "will to power." Reality in all its multifacetedness and complexity can never be construed or understood in a purely neutral or objective fashion. There is always

some presupposition or other at work. The Christian presupposition is that reality is about being in communion now, by
God's grace, and about being drawn into further and deeper
communion in the Divine Communion in every way God
wishes, but, *par excellence,* through the church and, therefore,
through its ministers, including deacons. This is self-donation.
All reach out to all to build up all as body of Christ in the
direction of the Parousia, but differently.

V

Perhaps I feel too passionately about the diaconate! There
should be no need for—but too often there is a need for—an
apologia for the diaconate. I hope these few words in response
to Bishop Campbell's wise words will help to advance the
apologetic. Ultimately, however, the best apologetic for the diaconate will be diaconal performance—holy deacons whose
holiness shines through their commitment to service, their
theological and evangelical intelligence, but especially through
their compassionate, loving presence in the church.

Notes

1. Edward P. Echlin, "The Origins of the Permanent
Deacon" (August 1970), 92–106.
2. (New York: The Seabury Press, 1968).
3. (New York: The Seabury Press, 1981).
4. (Collegeville: The Liturgical Press, 1985).

5. Paulist Press currently publishes the following titles on the diaconate: *Deacons and the Church* by Owen F. Cummings (2004); *101 Questions & Answers on Deacons* by William T. Ditewig (2004); *Saintly Deacons* by Owen F. Cummings (2005); *Theology of the Diaconate: The State of the Question* by Owen F. Cummings, William T. Ditewig, and Richard R. Gaillardetz (2005); and *Preach What You Believe: Timeless Homilies for Deacons—Cycle B* by Michael E. Bulson (2005).

6. (Washington, DC: USCCB, 2005).

7. (Chicago: Liturgical Training Publications, 2004).

8. *National Directory,* paragraph 239.

9. For a summary of John N. Collins's insights, see Owen F. Cummings, *Deacons and the Church* (Mahwah, NJ: Paulist Press, 2004), 31–34.

10. Owen F. Cummings, William T. Ditewig, and Richard R. Gaillardetz, *Theology of the Diaconate: State of the Question* (Mahwah, NJ: Paulist Press, 2005), 21–27.

11. Raymond E. Brown, SS, *An Introduction to the New Testament* (New York and London: Doubleday, 1997), 657.

12. Pope Benedict XVI, *Pilgrim Fellowship of Faith: The Church as Communion* (San Francisco: Ignatius Press, 2005), 140.

13. Peter E. Fink, SJ, *Praying the Sacraments* (Washington, DC: The Pastoral Press, 1991), 119.

14. Robert Barron, *Bridging the Great Divide* (Chicago: Rowman and Littlefield, 2004), 244–45.

Response to Deacon Ditewig: Community, Charism, and Competence

Marti R. Jewell

Director of Emerging Models of Pastoral Leadership
National Association for Lay Ministry

The work of formation is an art. It is also a science and a discipline. The role and skills of the formation director matter. So critical is it to the proper formation of a deacon that in 2005, the United States Bishops published a new *National Directory* designed to provide guidelines for this formation. The implementation of this *Directory,* and hence the charge of the deacon formation director, was the topic of a presentation by Deacon William Ditewig, Executive Director of the Secretariat for the Diaconate. I have been asked to respond to this presentation, and it is with pleasure that I accept this invitation.

As I approach the topic of the implementation of the *Directory*, I do so from the stance of more than fifteen years of directing diocesan ministry formation. Developing and working with ministry formation from the late 1980s, I began when there was little information about the work of the diocesan formation director. My specific charge was the formation of laity for ministry, although I also worked with deacon candidates. *How* to do this was the subject of intense interest and development across the United States. In the course of the past twenty years, much has been learned about this work, recognizing it as a discipline in itself.

I write, also, as Director of the "Emerging Models of Pastoral Leadership Project"[1] which is a joint project of the National Association of Diaconate Directors (NADD), the National Association for Lay Ministry (NALM), and four other national associations.[2] This project is conducting extensive research designed to understand how pastoral leadership is developing in today's parishes. As part of this research, the project is studying parish systems of leadership, systems in which pastors, deacons, lay ecclesial ministers, and parishioners work together to provide shared leadership in the parish. It is with this awareness of the role of the diaconate that I respond to Deacon Ditewig.

Addressing the development and implementation of the *2005 National Directory*, Ditewig speaks first of the role of the United States Bishops' Conference, and then of the development of the document, in which many dedicated people participated. Next, six elements are offered for consideration in the implementation of the *Directory*. The elements addressed involve interpretation, context, scope, content, attitude, and resources. These six suggest the scope of work given to the deacon formation director.

It is the charge of the deacon director and/or deacon formation director to walk with candidates through aspirancy, candidacy, and beyond. I would like to focus on three aspects of formation. Whether forming people for lay ministry, the priesthood, or the diaconate, these are critical tasks of the director. First is the task of assisting students in understanding and integrating into the community in which they will be ministering. I will focus on the formation of men— and often their wives—into the community of the diocese. This involves both the "Context: Link between Relationships and Structures" and "Scope: Diocesan Church" that Ditewig addresses.

Second, formation focuses on the person's relationship to God and the development of their God-given gifts and charisms. This involves the "Content: Current Process, Law, Policy," that is at the heart of the *National Directory*. How do deacon directors form the candidates into the spiritual and theological charism of the diaconate?

Third, those preparing for ministry need both knowledge and the ability to integrate that knowledge into their ministry. These are both addressed by the deacon standards that are a significant part of the *National Directory* and how they relate to other ministry standards in use, the "Resources" to which Ditewig refers. Each of these tasks, essential to the formation of the deacon, requires specific disciplines and skills on the part of the formation director.

Diocesan Community

Aspirants to the diaconate come to formation with a desire to be something or to do something they have seen in others and dreamed of for themselves. The same would be true in a person aspiring to priesthood or lay ecclesial ministry. The process of integrating or internalizing the diaconate is one that must be carefully guided by the formation director. There are recognizable steps in this process. When this formation is done well in lay ministry programs, people who arrived wanting to do ministry leave saying, "I am a minister." How does this apply to the diaconate?

We know that different professions have unique ways of initiating people into their new identity. Doctors have internships and residencies. Police pair junior officers with experienced ones. Priests, deacons, and lay ministers go through a particular formation process as well. How one scripts this movement is at the heart of the formation process. Each event, each course, each theological reflection, even when they happen relative to each other, impacts the formation experience of the aspirant or candidate.

The first step is the outer formation of the deacon candidate: *how* the person is formed or mentored into the community. This is a two-way street. Is the new deacon accepted and welcomed by the clerical and lay communities? Does the new deacon welcome the entire community into his life? According to the *National Directory,* "By virtue of their ordination, a sacramental fraternity unites deacons. They form a community that witnesses to Christ."[3] As Ditewig suggests:

> This sacramental relationship between the bishop and his deacons provides the context for the integration of the order of deacons into the pastoral life of the diocesan church.[4]

It is the role of the deacon director to move the candidate beyond the excitement of joining the deacon community and initiate them into the diocesan structures and larger community as well. The challenge then becomes one of aiding the newly formed deacon to accept those who are different from himself, and to have an understanding of the community at large.

> In his works of charity, the deacon guides and witnesses to the Church "the love of Christ for all [people] instead of personal interests and ideologies which are injurious to the universality of salvation...."[5]

According to Ditewig, "It is clear in the *Directory* that the bishops want there to be no confusion on this issue: deacons serve him in the whole diocesan church."[6] There are a number of methodologies available for inviting the candidates into a wider view of the diocese, from visiting a variety of parishes to ensuring that a variety of ecclesiological texts are required.

Diaconal Charism

The second task is the inner formation of the person, the development of the charism and gifts of the deacon. As the formation director seeks to understand and implement the content of the *Directory*, it is with one goal in mind: the formation of the deacon. At the heart of this formation is the development of the diaconal charism and gifts. As a lay ecclesial minister and formator, this is the area that I find most inviting about the diaconate. The formation director must provide the processes that will allow the candidate to develop this charism. Good formation does not attempt to instill a character that is not within a person to begin with, but enhances the gifts and call given to each individual. Formation is about structuring a process that enhances the encounter between God and the person. In that encounter persons come to recognize, claim, and use their gifts.

For the deacon this charism is the charism of service or charity. Contained in the phrase "being the presence of the church with the poor, and the voice of the poor in the church," an explanation of this charism is found in the *National Directory*. This is the hallmark of the faithfulness of the deacon.

In his formal liturgical roles, the deacon brings the poor to the Church and the Church to the poor. Likewise, he articulates the Church's concern for justice by being a driving force in addressing the injustices among God's people. He thus symbolizes in his roles the grounding of the Church's life in the Eucharist and the mission of the Church in her loving service of the needy.[7]

This is expressed powerfully, for me, in the stories of the experience of the German bishops sitting in the concentration camps of World War II. They had no power or authority in that place, and yet they found that their presence provided much needed comfort, prayer, and solace to those in the camp—this, the most basic of diaconal ministry. They discovered, in their own experience, how powerful it is to be the presence of the church with the poor.

There is no doubt about the gift and call of the diaconate. Many lines have been written to describe the apparently debated theology of the diaconate. Yet, deacons have been present since the beginnings of our tradition in the early church. The permanent diaconate, as it was understood by Vatican II, has its roots in scripture. In the Pauline writings, deacons—men and women—were present to and served the needs of the fledgling church.

Beyond scripture, both Vatican II and the 1983 *Code of Canon Law* state that deacons are ordained into the clerical state (c. 266.1). As clergy, they participate in the threefold *munera* of the bishop. Theirs is a ministry of word, worship, and charity. While *all* the faithful participate in their own way in these *munera* as priest, prophet, and king (c. 204), the deacons participate by virtue of both baptism and orders.

How this ministry is lived out, whether as leader or servant—or both—must be developed by each deacon. And yet, this clarity notwithstanding, I have witnessed the struggle of the deacon community to claim its place in the ecclesial structure. Even more so, it seems that the church itself is struggling to understand who and what a deacon is! The important work of developing a theology of the diaconate is underway. This discussion, however, must include practical considerations of roles and functions. These are areas that are not yet well understood in the church community. What are the roles the deacon is to fill? How does the deacon function in the diocesan and parish structure? How does the deacon relate to other ordained and lay ministers?

Where the deacon is serving in prisons, nursing homes, or shelters, there is little doubt about his role and charism. The deacon is there, with the poor, sent by the bishop who stands for the whole body of Christ. The deacon is the presence of the church to the poor! It is the second half of this call—to be the voice of the poor in the church—that appears to be less tangible.

In the documents the deacon is seen as a leader. This role flows from the understanding of the cleric as a leader, participating in the three *munera* of the church. As I listen to deacons across the country, it appears there is *no* consistent understanding of the role of the deacon in the parish. Some ministers speak of competition between deacons and lay ecclesial ministers in parishes. This confusion stems, at least in part, from confusion between the corporate understanding of leadership and that of the minister.

Culturally, "leader" is seen as the "one in charge." Americans have come to believe in the "hero-leader," the one who has all the answers and can do all things. "In today's organization, this idealization of great leadership leads to an endless search for heroic figures who can come in to rescue the rest of us from recalcitrant, non-competitive institutions."[8] But here is the rub: the deacon is called to be the voice of the *poor* in the church, thus embodying the tension inherent in church leadership. How does one understand the true meaning of the servanthood to which Jesus calls us in a world that combines the idea of leader with hero?

It is in the charism of the deacon that perhaps some resolution of this tension can be found. The deacon is called to let go of the corporate understanding of leadership and lead through this focus on the poor. "The deacon should recall that every action in the Church should be informed by charity and service to all...."[9] It is the call of the deacon to animate this charism at every turn.

> In his preaching and teaching, the deacon articulates the need and hopes of the people he has experienced [in his daily life], thereby animating,

motivating, and facilitating a commitment among the lay faithful to an evangelical service in the world.[10]

This is true leadership. This serves the church. Not an easy charism, to be sure, but it is a much needed one! Where this is done well, each parishioner would not only recognize the deacon, but would know the poor must be honored and will have a voice in their church. Each task taken on by the deacon must be colored by this charism. The deacon must animate this awareness in those around him. How does one do this? What kind of leader is the deacon to be? How does he live this out in a parish in a way that truly provides the poor with a voice? It is the work of the formation director to assist the candidate in learning to live within these tensions.

Ministerial Competencies

The third area I wish to address, ministerial competency, is perhaps the most recent of formation practices. Both the diaconate and lay ministry have moved forward with the development of competency-based standards for ministry. Both have a shared history of development beginning in the 1990s when representatives from national organizations and the Bishops' Conference gathered together to discover what competencies were and how they could be applied to preparing people for ministry.

Marti R. Jewell

The National Federation of Catholic Youth Ministers
(NFCYM) had taken the lead in this endeavor with their
publication of competencies for youth ministers. The
National Association for Lay Ministry (NALM) then developed competencies for pastoral associates, parish ministers,
and parish life coordinators (c. 517.2). Following them the
National Conference of Catechetical Leaders (NCCL) published competencies for directors of religious education.
These organizations continued to meet annually, along with
other organizations, which were also interested in developing ministerial competencies.

Then NADD board member Deacon Steve Graff was a
participant in these meetings and at this time the development of the competencies for deacons began. In this new
world of ministerial competency writing, competencies for
deacons were based on those already written by these
national organizations. Gradually, these competencies took
on their own shape and where approved by the United States
Bishops. Since then, a second generation of all of these competencies has developed. Those developed for deacons are
included in the *2005 National Directory.* Those developed
for the other organizations took a slightly different course.

Thanks to the work of people desiring to use the lay
ministry competencies to develop their formation programs
in the mid-1990s, it was discovered that the competencies of
NALM, NFCYM, and NCCL were not only similar, but in
many ways consistent even though the ministries were different. The three organizations decided to collaborate and,

after long hours of work, created competency-based ministry standards for those in ministry. These are now called "core ministry standards." A second layer of standards was then developed that are specific to different ministries and these are called "specialized standards."

> The core and specialized competencies distinguish the specific knowledge, skills, values, traits, or attitudes needed to fulfill the certification standards. The certification standards and core competencies are both foundational and common to all cited ministries. Specialized competencies address skills and responsibilities of a particular ministry that are either unique to that ministry or need to be expressed distinctly within the context of that ministry.[11]

Once it was recognized that similar competences, both knowledge and behavioral, were recognized for the different ministries, the competences began to be organized differently. The lay ministry competences were organized by theme. When they were approved by the USCCB Commission on Certification and Accreditation in 2003, the "National Certification Standards for Lay Ecclesial Ministry" were grouped in the following categories:

I. Certification Standard One: Personal and Spiritual Maturity

II. Certification Standard Two: Lay Ecclesial and Ministry Identity

III. Certification Standard Three: Catholic Theology

IV. Certification Standard Four: Pastoral Praxis

V. Certification Standard Five: Professional Practice

These standards were then developed with a vision statement for each, a listing of the knowledge required, accompanied by behavioral indicators. For each of the five standards there were also listed the specific competencies needed by the ministries for which the standards were written:

• Catechetical leaders
• Youth ministers
• Pastoral associates
• Parish life coordinators (c. 517.2)

These standards are also based on the assumption that a person holding these positions will have a graduate degree or equivalent.

Subsequently, the National Association for Lay Ministry (NALM) has added competencies for pastoral ministers, *National Certification Standards for Pastoral Ministers*.[12] These standards, approved in 2004, are based on the same schema, but are for those parish ministers or parishioners who are serving the parish, but do not have graduate level training.

The standards for diaconal ministry, found in the *National Directory,* developed somewhat differently. Called "Standards for Readiness," they fall into three categories:

    I. Model Standards for Readiness for Admission into the Aspirant Path

    II. Model Standards for Readiness for Admission into the Candidate Path

    III. Model Standards for Readiness for the Ordination and Post-Ordination Path

Each category is then subdivided into the human, spiritual, intellectual, and pastoral dimensions, followed by "Diaconal Vocation and Ministry." Both knowledge and behavioral indicators of that knowledge are listed for each dimension. As men progress through the three paths, the competences expected to meet the standards increase, or deepen, so that by the time a person is ordained, he is expected to have competence at the graduate or master's degree level.

Since the deacon standards were originally written with the pastoral associate standards in mind, it would not be difficult to correlate the two sets of standards. Hence it would serve the deacon formation director well to be familiar with both sets of standards. While the two schemas provide different entry points, the real gift to the church is the growing acceptance that when one accepts the responsibility of ministering with the people of God, there is a justified expectation of competence on the part of the minister.

There are practical implications of all of this for directors of diocesan deacon formation programs, as well as for those of lay ministry formation programs. Much discussion has taken place in this field about the feasibility of combining or not combining these programs. While there are very valid opinions both for and against this tact, they do not preclude the directors of these programs from collaborating and learning from one another. Those programs that are based on the standards, as deacon programs certainly must be, are not as far apart as they seem. The art of doing formation remains a constant, as well as an awareness of the responsibility to prepare competent ministers for the church.

It was to this end that Ditewig called for deacon formation directors to

> look beyond the obvious resources and see how we might be take advantage of all the expertise and experience that is out there just waiting to be tapped. This is also a great way to familiarize these other institutions and agencies with the nature and work of the diaconate itself; all can benefit from this mutual interaction.[13]

Conclusion

Men aspiring to the diaconate may not be aware of all three areas where they are in need of formation. Some come longing for community or the church of their past. Some may focus solely on how they will work in a parish. Others may think they are only going to serve the poor outside of the parameters of parish and diocesan life. None of these, by themselves, are options. When vowing obedience to their ordinary, they take on the full life of the deacon. Whether they see this role as leader or servant, they will be ordained into the community as deacon.

How well this happens depends on the skills of those charged with their formation. There are multiple competencies for formators themselves that are needed to accomplish this charge well. Formation directors need to know theories of adult formation and education, be able to use models for theological and self-reflection. They need to understand processes for supervising ministry and ministry students. These are just a few of the many skills needed. Fortunately, NADD offers training for directors. Other resources are available, such as the NALM Ministry Formation Director's Institute.[14]

We have much work to do to serve the parish community of the future. As the Emerging Models Project conducts its research, we are learning that emerging models of parish leadership are not focused on a single leader. They are developing in ways that provide the best possible leadership to stimulate vibrant and spiritually alive parish communities. The most energetic communities have a vision. Lay and ordained ministers work together in shared collaboration. Those leaders who do not see their parishes as vibrant may also speak of antiquated leadership models. As we begin to understand ourselves as total ministering communities, in which the gifts and competence of all—parishioners, staff, and clergy alike—are welcomed and empowered, we begin to understand the unique and necessary role of every member of the parish community.

The deacon role in this community is essential. Whether in their ministry of word, worship, or charity, the deacon brings us to the poor and the poor to us. To do this essential and challenging task, the deacon must be well formed, sure in his understanding and role as deacon, aware, competent, and able to use the gifts with which he has been endowed. He must hold the tension between servant and leader and so model and animate diaconal ministry of the church.

Notes

1. Emerging Models of Pastoral Leadership Project: www.emergingmodels.org.

2. Conference of Pastoral Planners and Council Development (CPPCD), National Association of Church Personnel Administrators (NACPA), National Federation of Priests' Councils (NFPC), and the National Catholic Young Adult Ministry Association.

3. *National Directory,* paragraph 54.

4. Ditewig, p. 44 herein.

5. *National Directory,* paragraph 57.

6. Ditewig, p. 45 herein.

7. *National Directory,* paragraph 37.

8. Peter M. Senge, "The Leadership of Profound Change." In *The Dance of Change,* Peter Senge et al. (New York: Doubleday, 1999), 11.

9. *National Directory,* paragraph 48.

10. *National Directory,* paragraph 58.

11. *National Certification Standards.* NFCYM, NALM, NCCL (Washington, DC, 2003), ix.

12. *National Certification Standards for Pastoral Ministers.* National Association for Lay Ministry (Washington, DC, 2004).

13. Ditewig, p. 51 herein.

14. www.nalm.org.